LIV MORGAN

Biography of Wrestling's Rising Star and Her Unstoppable Path to WWE Glory

Cody L. Sage

Copyright © 2025 Cody L. Sage.

All rights reserved. No part of this publication may be reproduced, stored in a retrieval system, or transmitted in any form or by any means, electronic, mechanical, photocopying, recording, or otherwise, without prior written permission of the author.

Disclaimer:

This biography is based on available sources and personal recollections. While accuracy has been prioritized, some events and details may be reconstructed or subject to interpretation. Readers are encouraged to cross-verify facts and consult multiple sources for a comprehensive understanding.

Table of Contents

Chapter 1
A Star Is Born
Early struggles and her journey to WWE

Chapter 2
Breaking into WWE
The WWE Tryouts: Proving Herself
Becoming Liv Morgan
A Rising Star

Chapter 3
The Riot Squad Era
The End of the Riot Squad

Chapter 4
Reinventing Liv Morgan
Life after the Riot Squad
A New Persona Begins to Emerge

    The Lana and Bobby Lashley Storyline

    Evolving Her In-Ring Style

    Connecting with the WWE Universe

Chapter 5

    The Road to Championship Gold

    The Money in the Bank Opportunity

    Defining Moments as a Champion

Chapter 6

    Setbacks and Comebacks

    The Physical Toll of Wrestling

    Reinventing Herself Once Again

Chapter 7

    Liv Morgan: Professional Career from 2023 to Present

    2023: Redemption and Tag Team Success

    2024: The Revenge Tour

    2024–2025: Championship Glory and High-Stakes Rivalries

Chapter 8

Beyond the Ring

    Liv's personal life and passions

    Passions Outside Wrestling

    Beyond the Ring: The Future

Chapter 1

A Star Is Born

Early struggles and her journey to WWE

The sun had just dipped below the horizon, casting a soft amber glow over Elmwood Park, New Jersey. In a modest home nestled within the town's quiet streets, a young Gionna Jene Daddio sat cross-legged on the living room floor. The sound of the television blared in the background, but her focus was laser-sharp. Her wide, expressive eyes were glued to the screen as larger-than-life figures grappled, leaped, and slammed each other in a spectacle of athleticism and storytelling. It was WWE, and it felt like magic.

For Gionna, this wasn't just entertainment. This was an escape—a portal to a world where underdogs could triumph, where passion and grit overcame the odds. She didn't just watch wrestling; she lived it. As her siblings laughed and roughhoused around her, she often found herself imitating the moves, her small frame attempting clumsy dropkicks and elbow drops onto cushions and pillows. Little did anyone know, these moments were the seeds of a dream that would one day bloom into reality.

Growing up wasn't easy for Gionna. Born on June 8, 1994, she was one of six siblings in a family that faced its fair share of hardships. Her father's absence meant her mother had to juggle multiple jobs to make ends meet. The Daddio household was far from affluent, but it was rich in love and resilience. Gionna learned early on that nothing in life would be handed to her.

Money was tight, and luxuries like wrestling merchandise or attending live shows were out of the question. But Gionna found ways to immerse herself in the world she loved. She'd watch wrestling videos on borrowed DVDs and stayed up late catching episodes of Monday Night Raw. Wrestling wasn't just a passion—it was her sanctuary, her reminder that even in the face of adversity, it was possible to rise.

As she navigated her teenage years, Gionna began to realize that wrestling wasn't just a fleeting interest. It was her calling. But dreams of stepping into the ring seemed impossibly far away. How could a girl from a small New Jersey town, with no connections and limited resources, ever hope to make it to WWE?

Despite her doubts, Gionna's natural charisma and unyielding determination began to shine. She found work at Hooters as a waitress, where her bubbly personality and tireless work ethic earned her recognition. Yet, the spark of wrestling never faded. Instead, it grew brighter. Every free moment was spent watching matches, studying moves, and envisioning herself under the bright lights of a WWE arena.

In 2014, Gionna's life took an unexpected turn. A chance encounter at a gym with a WWE talent scout changed everything. Recognizing her natural athleticism and magnetic energy, the scout encouraged her to audition. For Gionna, this was the moment she had been waiting for—a crack in the door to her dreams.

The WWE tryout was grueling, testing not just physical ability but mental toughness. Gionna was surrounded by seasoned athletes, many with years of wrestling experience. Yet, she refused to let intimidation get the better of her. Drawing on the resilience she had developed throughout her life, she pushed herself to the limit, showing off her agility, strength, and willingness to learn.

Transforming into Liv Morgan
When WWE offered her a developmental contract, Gionna's world changed overnight. Moving to Orlando, Florida, to train at the WWE Performance Center was both exhilarating and daunting. She was now part of a select group, but the journey ahead was steep.

Under the guidance of seasoned trainers, Gionna transformed into Liv Morgan, a character that mirrored her real-life tenacity and spunk. Inspired by her own journey, Liv Morgan became the embodiment of grit, a persona that fans would come to love for her authenticity and never-say-die attitude.

The road to WWE superstardom wasn't without its challenges. Liv had to learn the technical aspects of wrestling, develop her mic skills, and find her place in an industry dominated by larger-than-life personalities. But if her childhood had taught her anything, it was that persistence pays off.

As she stood in the Performance Center, drenched in sweat but with a fire in her eyes, she knew she was exactly where she was meant to be. Wrestling wasn't just a career—it was her destiny.

The journey from a small-town girl in New Jersey to a rising WWE star had only just begun. Liv Morgan's story was far from over. In fact, it was only getting started. The stage was set, the lights were bright, and the world was waiting to see what she would do next.

Chapter 2

Breaking into WWE

The fluorescent lights in the gym cast a stark glare over the rows of equipment, but Gionna Jene Daddio wasn't paying attention to her surroundings. She was focused on her form, the weights in her hands, and the rhythm of her workout. It was just another day in her relentless pursuit of staying fit, another step in the disciplined life she had cultivated. But on this ordinary day in 2014, fate intervened. A WWE talent scout, drawn to her athletic build and undeniable charisma, approached her with a life-changing proposition: an invitation to audition for WWE.

For Gionna, this was the moment she had dreamed of since childhood, a golden opportunity to step into the world that had captivated her for so long. Yet, excitement was quickly replaced by nerves. Could she truly stand out among the hundreds of hopefuls vying for the same chance?

The WWE Tryouts: Proving Herself

The WWE tryouts were a battleground where only the strongest and most determined survived. Held over several grueling days, these auditions tested physical ability, mental toughness, and charisma. Gionna arrived in Orlando with nothing but her determination and the raw athleticism she had honed over years of hard work.

Surrounded by seasoned athletes, former football players, gymnasts, and even indie wrestlers, Gionna felt like an underdog. She had no prior wrestling experience, no flashy accolades to boast about. But what she lacked in credentials, she made up for with grit.

The drills were intense—sprints, weightlifting, and endurance exercises designed to push participants to their limits. Then came the ring work: running the ropes, taking bumps, and learning the basics of wrestling. Every fall left her body aching, but she refused to let the pain show.

Perhaps most daunting were the promo sessions, where hopefuls were required to step in front of a camera and deliver a speech with the charisma of a WWE Superstar. Gionna dug deep, channeling the boldness she had cultivated during her years as a waitress at Hooters, where she had learned to handle any situation with confidence.

By the end of the tryouts, Gionna's relentless spirit and undeniable potential had caught the attention of WWE officials. She had passed the test, earning a coveted developmental contract and a spot at the WWE Performance Center.

Moving to Orlando, Florida, to train at the WWE Performance Center was both a dream come true and an overwhelming challenge. The state-of-the-art facility was a haven for aspiring wrestlers, equipped with multiple rings, strength and conditioning equipment, and a team of world-class trainers. But for Gionna, it also symbolized the start of an uphill battle.

Every day at the Performance Center was a test of endurance and adaptability. The morning started with rigorous physical training—weightlifting, cardio, and injury prevention exercises. Afternoons were dedicated to learning in-ring techniques, from grappling and submission holds to perfecting the art of storytelling through wrestling. Evenings often involved promo classes, where trainees were coached on how to captivate an audience with their words.

Gionna's initial lack of wrestling experience meant she had to work twice as hard as her peers. But her natural athleticism and unyielding determination quickly set her apart. She soaked up every piece of advice, every critique, and every ounce of wisdom from her trainers like a sponge.

Becoming Liv Morgan

Wrestling is as much about character as it is about athleticism. In the world of WWE, your persona is your identity, the bridge between you and the audience. For Gionna, creating her character was a journey of self-discovery.

Drawing from her own experiences and personality, she crafted the persona of Liv Morgan. Liv was spunky, rebellious, and unapologetically herself—a reflection of the tough, resilient girl from Elmwood Park who had fought her way to WWE. Her character was relatable yet captivating, a mix of grit and charm that resonated with fans.

Liv's look was equally distinctive. Her platinum blonde hair, street-style attire, and mischievous grin set her apart from the rest of the women's roster. Her entrance music, upbeat and defiant, became a soundtrack for her journey.

Despite her rapid growth, Liv's journey was far from smooth. The competitive environment of the Performance Center meant she constantly had to prove herself. Mistakes were inevitable, and every misstep felt magnified under the watchful eyes of trainers and peers.

Liv also had to navigate the emotional toll of being away from home. Her family had always been her anchor, and now she was miles away, navigating a demanding career on her own. But every setback only fueled her determination to succeed.

A Rising Star

Months of hard work began to pay off as Liv started making appearances on WWE's developmental brand, NXT. Her debut was electric—she brought a fresh energy to the women's division, quickly earning a reputation as a scrappy underdog. Fans were drawn to her authenticity and infectious enthusiasm, making her a standout even in a roster filled with talent.

Her time in NXT was a critical period of growth. Liv refined her in-ring style, blending agility and high-energy moves that matched her personality. She also began forming connections with fans, who admired her resilience and relatability.

By the time Liv Morgan's name started gaining traction in NXT, it was clear that Gionna Jene Daddio had transformed into a bona fide WWE Superstar. Her journey from an ordinary girl in New Jersey to a rising star in the wrestling world was a testament to the power of determination and self-belief.

Liv Morgan wasn't just a character—she was a symbol of perseverance, someone who had clawed her way into a world where dreams often felt out of reach. And while her journey was only beginning, one thing was certain: Liv Morgan was here to stay.

Chapter 3

The Riot Squad Era

The lights in the arena dimmed, and an eerie silence filled the air. Suddenly, the sound of glass shattering gave way to a hard-hitting rock anthem. Three women stormed down the ramp with a sense of urgency, their expressions unyielding and fierce. Among them was Liv Morgan, her signature platinum blonde hair catching the strobe lights as she grinned with mischievous confidence. Flanked by Ruby Riott, the tattooed leader with a punk-rock edge, and Sarah Logan, the rugged powerhouse, the trio exuded an undeniable presence. This was the Riot Squad, and they were here to shake up WWE's women's division.

By late 2017, WWE was undergoing a revolution in women's wrestling. The Women's Evolution was in full swing, with female Superstars headlining events, competing in groundbreaking matches, and reshaping the industry's perception of women's roles in sports entertainment. For Liv Morgan, it was the perfect time to take her career to the next level.

Liv had made her mark in NXT as a scrappy underdog, but her main roster debut came with a twist. On November 21, 2017, Liv joined forces with Ruby Riott and Sarah Logan to form the Riot Squad, a rebellious faction set on causing chaos. The group was positioned as disruptors, targeting established stars like Charlotte Flair, Naomi, and Becky Lynch.

The dynamic between the three women was electric. Ruby, the vocal leader, brought a raw intensity and vision to the group. Sarah, with her Viking-inspired persona, added brute strength and unpredictability. Liv, the youngest and most exuberant member, brought a spark of mischief and energy that balanced the trio. Together, they were a force to be reckoned with.

The Riot Squad made an unforgettable debut on SmackDown Live, attacking Naomi and Becky Lynch in a shocking display of dominance. The segment set the tone for their run—a chaotic blend of rebellion and ruthlessness. Liv thrived in this environment, embracing her role as the wild card of the group.

The trio's mission was clear: to dismantle the hierarchy of WWE's women's division. They targeted everyone from fan favorites to authority figures, leaving destruction in their wake. Their backstage segments, where they trashed locker rooms and played pranks, showcased their penchant for anarchy.

While the Riot Squad initially made waves with their antics, they soon had to prove themselves in the ring. Liv's high-energy style complemented Ruby's technical prowess and Sarah's raw power, making them a versatile team. Together, they competed in tag matches and six-woman tag bouts, often facing top-tier competitors.

Liv's growth during this time was evident. She began experimenting with her in-ring arsenal, incorporating moves like the springboard dropkick and her signature ObLivion. Her chemistry with Ruby and Sarah also deepened, creating seamless teamwork that allowed them to stand out in a crowded roster.

Despite their rebellious nature, the Riot Squad resonated with fans. Their authenticity and chemistry made them relatable, even as they played the heels. Liv, in particular, garnered attention for her unorthodox style and infectious energy, endearing her to the WWE Universe.

The Riot Squad's journey wasn't without its challenges. In an era dominated by iconic stars like Charlotte Flair, Sasha Banks, and Alexa Bliss, carving out a lasting legacy was no easy feat. The group often found themselves on the losing end of matches, their momentum stifled by the dominance of the division's top names.

Despite these setbacks, the Riot Squad remained a cohesive unit. They continued to evolve, refining their characters and in-ring performances. Liv, in particular, used this period to develop her skills and confidence, preparing herself for the next chapter of her career.

The Riot Squad's run was punctuated by several standout moments. Their feud with Charlotte Flair, Becky Lynch, and Naomi showcased their potential as both antagonists and performers. In 2018, the group participated in the first-ever women's Royal Rumble match, a historic milestone in WWE history.

Liv's performances in these matches highlighted her growth as a competitor. She wasn't just a background player—she was a vital part of the action, earning her place among the division's rising stars.

The End of the Riot Squad

By mid-2019, cracks began to form within the Riot Squad. WWE's decision to split the group during the Superstar Shake-Up saw Ruby Riott and Sarah Logan moved to different brands, leaving Liv on her own. The dissolution of the Riot Squad marked the end of an era, but it also signaled the beginning of Liv's journey as a solo competitor.

While the group's time together was relatively short-lived, their impact was undeniable. The Riot Squad had carved out a unique niche in WWE's women's division, providing a platform for Liv Morgan to showcase her talent and personality.

The Riot Squad was more than just a faction—it was a proving ground for Liv Morgan. The experience of working alongside Ruby Riott and Sarah Logan helped her grow as a performer, teaching her the importance of chemistry, storytelling, and adaptability.

As Liv prepared to embark on her solo career, the lessons learned during the Riot Squad era would prove invaluable. She was no longer the wide-eyed rookie from Elmwood Park—she was a seasoned competitor, ready to take on the world.

The Riot Squad may have disbanded, but their spirit of rebellion and unity lived on in Liv

Morgan. Her journey was far from over, and the best was yet to come.

Chapter 4

Reinventing Liv Morgan

Life after the Riot Squad

The crowd noise faded into a low hum as Liv Morgan stood backstage, peeking through the curtain at the WWE arena. It had been months since the Riot Squad had dissolved, leaving her to navigate uncharted waters as a solo competitor. The safety net of Ruby Riott and Sarah Logan was gone, and with it, the identity she had leaned on since her debut. Now, it was just her—Liv Morgan—alone and ready to prove she was more than a supporting player in a faction.

This wasn't just a new chapter in her career. It was a rebirth.

When the Riot Squad disbanded in 2019, Liv Morgan found herself in a challenging position. As a member of a faction, she had enjoyed a certain level of visibility and support. On her own, she was forced to carve out a space in WWE's stacked women's division, where competition was fierce, and opportunities were scarce.

Her first solo appearances were sporadic, and for a while, it seemed as though Liv was struggling to find her footing. She participated in matches on Monday Night Raw and SmackDown, but her character lacked the depth and direction needed to make a lasting impression. The WWE

Universe began to wonder: what's next for Liv Morgan?

Behind the scenes, Liv was grappling with the same question. Determined to reinvent herself, she threw herself into training, honing her skills and experimenting with her in-ring style. Liv's athleticism had always been her strength, but now she was working to become a more well-rounded performer, both in the ring and on the mic.

A New Persona Begins to Emerge

In late 2019, WWE began teasing a reinvention for Liv Morgan. Vignettes aired showing Liv in a reflective, vulnerable state, speaking about rediscovering who she truly was. The segments were cryptic but compelling, hinting at a deeper, more complex character than fans had seen before.

When Liv finally returned to WWE television in early 2020, it was clear that she had undergone a transformation. Gone was the mischievous, rebellious persona from her Riot Squad days. In its place was a more polished and confident Liv Morgan, one who seemed ready to embrace her individuality and step into the spotlight.

Her revamped look—sleek attire, a refined entrance, and a fresh aura of determination—signaled her intent to stand out. WWE was giving her a chance to prove herself as a solo star, and Liv wasn't about to let it slip away.

The Lana and Bobby Lashley Storyline

Liv's return was marked by her involvement in a controversial storyline with Lana and Bobby Lashley. During Lana and Lashley's wedding segment on Monday Night Raw, Liv interrupted the ceremony, revealing that she and Lana had a romantic past. The moment was shocking, divisive, and instantly went viral, putting Liv back in the spotlight.

Though the storyline itself received mixed reactions, it served as a platform for Liv to showcase her improved mic skills and emotional range. She brought a sense of vulnerability and intensity to her performances, reminding fans of her versatility as a performer.

More importantly, the storyline marked the beginning of Liv's evolution as a solo competitor. WWE had taken notice of her potential, and the Lana-Lashley angle was a stepping stone to bigger opportunities.

<u>Evolving Her In-Ring Style</u>

As Liv began competing regularly again, it became clear that her in-ring style had undergone a transformation as well. She incorporated new moves into her arsenal, blending agility and technical precision with her trademark energy.

One of her most notable additions was her finishing move, ObLivion, a rope-assisted flatliner that showcased her creativity and athleticism. Liv's matches were fast-paced and dynamic, reflecting her growth as a performer.

Her feud with Ruby Riott in mid-2020 provided her with an opportunity to tell a compelling story in the ring. The former Riot Squad members clashed in emotional matches, with Liv emerging as a confident and capable solo competitor.

Connecting with the WWE Universe

One of Liv's greatest strengths has always been her ability to connect with fans. Her authenticity and relatability set her apart in an industry often defined by larger-than-life personas.

During this period of reinvention, Liv leaned into her connection with the WWE Universe.

She was open about her journey on social media, sharing her struggles and triumphs with her followers. Fans responded with overwhelming support, rallying behind her as she worked to establish herself as a star.

Liv's relatability wasn't just about her personal story—it was about her message. She became a symbol of resilience and self-discovery, inspiring fans to embrace their individuality and chase their dreams.

By late 2020, it was clear that Liv Morgan's reinvention was paying off. She had established herself as a solo competitor, delivering strong performances in the ring and earning the respect of her peers.

Her matches with top-tier talent like Charlotte Flair, Asuka, and Sasha Banks proved that she could hold her own against the best in the division. Liv wasn't just surviving—she was thriving, proving that she was more than capable of being a standout star.

Reinventing herself wasn't an easy process, but Liv Morgan had emerged stronger, more confident, and more determined than ever. She had faced the uncertainty of life after the Riot Squad and turned it into an opportunity to grow, evolve, and shine.

As she stood in the center of the ring, her hand raised in victory after another hard-fought match, it was clear that Liv's journey was far from over. The WWE Universe wasn't just watching a wrestler—they were witnessing the rise of a star.

For Liv Morgan, the future was bright. And the best was yet to come.

Chapter 5

The Road to Championship Gold

The roar of the crowd was deafening, the energy in the arena palpable. Liv Morgan stood in the middle of the ring, her chest heaving from the grueling match she had just endured. Clutched in her hands was the object of her lifelong dream—the WWE SmackDown Women's Championship. Tears streamed down her face as she hoisted the title high above her head, the culmination of years of perseverance, hard work, and self-belief. This moment wasn't just a victory; it was the validation of her journey.

But the road to this defining moment had been anything but easy.

After years of building her reputation as a dependable and versatile performer, Liv Morgan began her ascent to championship contention in 2021. Her solo journey following the dissolution of the Riot Squad had showcased her potential, but the competitive nature of WWE's women's division meant breaking into the upper echelon required something extraordinary.

Liv's breakout moment came during her rivalry with Carmella and Zelina Vega. These feuds allowed her to display her grit and determination, earning her a growing fan base that rallied behind her underdog story. Liv's performances were marked by her fiery resilience, and her ability to sell both her physicality and emotional investment made her matches compelling to watch.

The Money in the Bank Opportunity

The 2022 Money in the Bank ladder match became the turning point in Liv Morgan's career. A match synonymous with chaos and unpredictability, it offered the winner a guaranteed championship opportunity at a time of their choosing. For Liv, it was the chance to take her destiny into her own hands.

The match was a showcase of Liv's growth as a competitor. She battled some of the division's top stars, including Becky Lynch, Asuka, and Alexa Bliss. Despite the odds, Liv displayed incredible athleticism and ring awareness, seizing the briefcase in a heart-pounding finale that left fans erupting in cheers.

This victory wasn't just a win; it was a statement. Liv Morgan was no longer the scrappy underdog on the fringes of the roster—she was a legitimate threat in the women's division, ready to take her place among the elite.

Liv's Money in the Bank win set the stage for one of the most emotional moments in her career. Later that same night, Ronda Rousey successfully defended her SmackDown Women's Championship. As Ronda celebrated her victory, Liv's music hit, and the crowd exploded with anticipation.

Clutching her briefcase, Liv sprinted to the ring, cashing in her contract for an impromptu title match. The tension in the arena was electric as Liv pinned Ronda in a swift, dramatic sequence.

When the referee's hand hit the mat for the three-count, Liv Morgan became the new SmackDown Women's Champion.

The arena erupted in a deafening cheer as Liv fell to her knees, overwhelmed with emotion. It was the moment she had worked for her entire life—a moment of triumph that solidified her as a top-tier Superstar in WWE.

Defining Moments as a Champion

Winning the championship was one thing; defending it was another. Liv's reign as SmackDown Women's Champion was a testament to her resilience and adaptability. Her first major title defense came against Ronda Rousey at SummerSlam 2022. The match was a high-stakes encounter, pitting Liv's scrappiness against Ronda's unparalleled MMA background.

Though controversial due to the match's ending, Liv retained her title, proving her mettle as a fighting champion. The WWE Universe continued to rally behind her, drawn to her authenticity and never-give-up attitude.

Another standout moment of her reign came during her rivalry with Shayna Baszler. Known for her ruthless submission style, Shayna posed a formidable challenge. Liv's match against Shayna at Clash at the Castle showcased her evolution as a competitor, as she combined technical prowess with sheer determination to secure a hard-fought victory.

Throughout her championship reign, Liv's connection with the fans deepened. Her story resonated with the WWE Universe, particularly those who saw themselves in her journey. Liv wasn't a towering powerhouse or a decorated athlete with a storied background. She was a dreamer who had clawed her way to the top through grit and determination.

Her interactions with fans, both on-screen and off, further cemented her status as one of WWE's most beloved Superstars. Even if it was through heartfelt promos or social media posts, Liv consistently expressed her gratitude for the support she received, making her reign feel like a shared victory.

Liv's reign as champion wasn't without its challenges. Criticism from detractors, intense pressure to perform, and the physical toll of defending her title all tested her resolve. But each obstacle became a learning experience, shaping her into a more confident and capable performer.

Although her reign eventually came to an end, Liv walked away with her head held high, knowing she had given everything she had. She had proven to herself—and the world—that she belonged in the spotlight.

Liv Morgan's journey to championship gold was a story of perseverance, self-discovery, and triumph. From her humble beginnings in Elmwood Park, New Jersey, to the grand stage of WWE, Liv's path was defined by her ability to overcome adversity and embrace her individuality.

As a champion, she not only elevated herself but also inspired countless fans to chase their own dreams, no matter how daunting the odds. Liv Morgan's road to championship gold was a testament to the power of determination, and her story continues to inspire the next generation of WWE Superstars.

For Liv, the championship wasn't the end of the journey—it was a new beginning. The climb to the top had prepared her for even greater heights, and the WWE Universe eagerly awaited what was next for the girl who turned her dreams into reality.

Chapter 6

Setbacks and Comebacks

The crowd erupted into cheers as Liv Morgan stepped onto the ramp, her signature grin lighting up the arena. Yet, behind the infectious energy and confident demeanor was a woman who had weathered countless storms, both physical and emotional. Liv's journey to this moment was not without its share of challenges, setbacks, and heartbreaks. For every victory she celebrated, there were battles fought in silence, away from the bright lights of the WWE stage.

Her story was a testament to resilience—a narrative of how adversity can forge strength and how setbacks can become the foundation for comebacks.

The Physical Toll of Wrestling

Professional wrestling is as punishing as it is exhilarating. The high-flying maneuvers, the bone-crunching slams, and the relentless travel schedule all take a toll on the body. For Liv Morgan, the grind of being a WWE Superstar was both a dream fulfilled and a daily challenge.

In the years following her main roster debut, Liv faced her share of injuries. Minor sprains, bruises, and nagging pains were part of the job, but more significant injuries tested her resilience. One such incident occurred during a tag team match when Liv suffered a concussion after an accidental kick to the head.

The injury sidelined her temporarily, forcing her to confront the reality of life outside the ring. For someone who had dedicated her life to wrestling, being unable to perform was a devastating blow. Liv described the experience as "isolating," a period marked by frustration and self-doubt. Yet, even in those dark moments, she found ways to push forward.

The physical pain of injuries was compounded by the emotional toll of being sidelined. In an industry where visibility is everything, extended absences can sometimes feel like a career death sentence. Liv feared being forgotten by fans and overlooked by WWE management.

During her recovery, she turned to her support system, which included her family, friends, and fellow WWE Superstars. Their encouragement reminded her of her own resilience, and she began channeling her frustration into motivation. Liv dedicated herself to physical therapy, using the time away from the ring to not only heal but also improve.

She also focused on her mental health, recognizing the importance of staying positive and mentally strong. Meditation, journaling, and setting small, achievable goals became part of her routine. Liv's time away from wrestling became an opportunity for growth—a chance to refine her skills, rebuild her confidence, and come back stronger than ever.

<u>Reinventing Herself Once Again</u>

When Liv returned to WWE, she was determined to make an impact. She knew she couldn't simply pick up where she left off; she needed to evolve.

Her comeback matches showcased a sharper, more refined Liv Morgan. She had worked on her technical skills during her time away, adding new moves to her repertoire and improving her ring psychology. Fans noticed the change—this was a Liv Morgan who was hungrier, more focused, and ready to take her career to the next level.

Her return was marked by a series of compelling matches and rivalries, each one serving as a reminder of her resilience. Even if facing off against veterans like Charlotte Flair or newer stars like Bianca Belair, Liv brought a level of intensity and determination that resonated with fans.

One of the most defining aspects of Liv's career has been her ability to turn adversity into strength. Injuries, losses, and career setbacks have all served as opportunities for her to grow and evolve.

Her journey resonated deeply with fans who saw themselves in her struggles. Liv became a symbol of perseverance, a reminder that setbacks are not the end but rather a chance to start anew. Her authenticity—her willingness to share both her triumphs and her challenges—only deepened her connection with the WWE Universe.

A Turning Point: The Liv Morgan We Know Today

In 2022, Liv faced another setback when a knee injury temporarily derailed her momentum. This time, however, she approached her recovery with the wisdom of someone who had been through it all before.

Instead of succumbing to frustration, Liv used the time to reflect on her journey and refine her goals. She emerged from her recovery with a renewed sense of purpose, vowing to take her career to new heights. Her return was met with an outpouring of support from fans, who celebrated her resilience and cheered her on as she continued to chase her dreams.

Liv Morgan's setbacks didn't define her; her comebacks did. Each injury, each loss, and each moment of doubt became a stepping stone toward greater achievements. Her story is one of transformation—of how adversity can become the catalyst for growth and how strength is often forged in the fire of challenges.

Today, Liv stands as a symbol of perseverance in WWE. Her journey serves as a reminder that even when the odds seem insurmountable, it's possible to rise, stronger and more determined than ever.

As she looks toward the future, Liv knows that setbacks are inevitable, but they no longer intimidate her. She's proven time and time again that she has what it takes to not only overcome challenges but to thrive in their aftermath.

The girl from Elmwood Park who dreamed of becoming a WWE Superstar has become so much more than that. She's a fighter, a role model, and a testament to the power of resilience. And for Liv Morgan, the best is always yet to come.

Chapter 7

Liv Morgan: Professional Career from 2023 to Present

Following her explosive rise to prominence in 2022 with her Money in the Bank victory and first championship reign, Liv Morgan continued to evolve her persona and career trajectory in WWE. Her blend of resilience, emotional depth, and raw determination has made her a standout performer in the women's division.

2023: Redemption and Tag Team Success

Liv Morgan kicked off 2023 in remarkable fashion at the Royal Rumble on January 28, entering at #2 and lasting a record-breaking 1:01:07, only to be eliminated last by Rhea Ripley. This effort solidified Morgan as a cornerstone of the division. At Elimination Chamber in February, she delivered another standout performance, although she was eliminated in a hard-fought match.

Transitioning into the tag team division, Morgan teamed with Raquel Rodriguez. Their partnership quickly bore fruit as they won the WWE Women's Tag Team Championship on the April 10 episode of Raw by defeating Becky Lynch and Lita. Their reign, though compelling, was cut short when Morgan suffered a shoulder injury, leading to the titles being vacated in May. Undeterred, Morgan returned at Money in the Bank on July 1, reclaiming the Tag Team Championship alongside Rodriguez after capitalizing on Shayna Baszler's betrayal of Ronda Rousey. However, their reign ended swiftly due to backstage interference by Rhea Ripley, leading to a storyline injury for Morgan that sidelined her again.

2024: The Revenge Tour

Liv Morgan made her triumphant return at the 2024 Royal Rumble, entering at #30 and once again achieving runner-up status after an electrifying performance. Following this, she participated in the Elimination Chamber, where she was the last woman eliminated by Becky Lynch.

Morgan's return marked the beginning of a more aggressive and villainous persona. In April, she attacked Rhea Ripley backstage, inadvertently causing Ripley to vacate the Women's World Championship. This rivalry took a turn at King and Queen of the Ring, where Morgan defeated Lynch to claim the title, aided by accidental interference from Dominik Mysterio. This marked Morgan's second reign as champion and the start of her storyline association with Mysterio, culminating in a steel cage victory over Lynch on Raw and a dramatic on-screen kiss with Mysterio, officially aligning her with The Judgment Day faction.

At SummerSlam, Morgan retained her title against Ripley with Dominik's assistance, marking Ripley's first pinfall loss in over a year. This victory cemented Morgan's heel turn and her membership in The Judgment Day. Despite losing a mixed tag match to Ripley and Damian Priest at Bash in Berlin, Morgan's alliance with

Dominik and growing influence in The Judgment Day kept her at the center of WWE's most compelling stories.

2024–2025: Championship Glory and High-Stakes Rivalries

In November, Morgan captured the inaugural WWE Women's Crown Jewel Championship by defeating Nia Jax at Crown Jewel, adding another accolade to her growing legacy. Despite failing to recapture the Women's Tag Team Championship alongside Rodriguez, Morgan showcased her versatility by participating in a WarGames match at Survivor Series WarGames. Though her team fell short, Morgan's performance underscored her tenacity and willingness to adapt.

At Saturday Night's Main Event in December, Morgan successfully defended her Crown Jewel Championship against Iyo Sky, closing the year with momentum and further solidifying her status as a top-tier talent.

Chapter 8

Beyond the Ring

Liv's personal life and passions

Under the bright lights of the WWE stage, Liv Morgan is a fearless competitor, a charismatic performer, and a fan-favorite Superstar. But beyond the ring, there's another side to Liv—one defined by her personal passions, close relationships, and a deep connection with her fans. Gionna Jene Daddio, the woman behind Liv Morgan, is as multidimensional and captivating as the character she portrays on-screen.

Born and raised in Elmwood Park, New Jersey, Liv Morgan grew up in a close-knit family of six siblings. Despite facing financial hardships and the absence of her father, Liv's childhood was filled with love and resilience. Her mother worked tirelessly to provide for the family, instilling in Liv a strong work ethic and an appreciation for the value of hard work.

Away from the spotlight, Liv is deeply connected to her family, often referring to her siblings as her greatest support system. Their bond remains unshakable, even as her career takes her around the world. Liv frequently shares glimpses of her family life on social media, showcasing her roots and the people who have shaped her journey.

When she's not traveling for WWE, Liv enjoys a range of hobbies that reflect her dynamic personality. She's an animal lover with a particular fondness for her pet pig, who often makes appearances on her Instagram. Liv's playful and adventurous spirit shines through her love for outdoor activities, including hiking, fishing, and horseback riding.

Liv is also a passionate advocate for self-care and mental health. She has openly discussed her struggles with self-doubt and anxiety, using her platform to encourage fans to prioritize their well-being. Her honesty and vulnerability have made her relatable to many, reinforcing her status as a role model.

Passions Outside Wrestling

Liv's interests extend beyond wrestling and into the realms of fashion, fitness, and creative expression. Known for her edgy and ever-evolving style, Liv has become a trendsetter in WWE. Her outfits, often blending streetwear with high fashion, reflect her individuality and creativity. Fans frequently look to her for inspiration, and she has expressed interest in collaborating with designers or launching her own clothing line in the future.

Fitness remains a cornerstone of Liv's lifestyle. As a professional athlete, she is dedicated to maintaining her physical health, but she approaches fitness with balance and mindfulness. Liv often shares her workout routines and nutrition tips with fans, emphasizing the importance of staying active while also enjoying life.

Another passion close to her heart is acting. Liv has expressed a desire to explore opportunities in Hollywood, drawing inspiration from WWE Superstars like Dwayne "The Rock" Johnson and John Cena, who successfully transitioned to acting. Liv's charisma and ability to convey emotion make her a natural fit for roles in film or television, and fans eagerly anticipate what she might achieve in this realm.

Liv Morgan's connection with the WWE Universe is one of the most defining aspects of her career. From her early days in the Riot Squad to her championship reign, Liv has built a loyal fan base that resonates with her authenticity, relatability, and underdog spirit.

Liv actively engages with her fans on social media, sharing behind-the-scenes glimpses of her life, heartfelt messages, and playful interactions. Her ability to connect with people on a personal level has made her one of the most beloved Superstars in WWE. Even if it's responding to fan art, retweeting messages of support, or participating in charity events, Liv consistently shows her gratitude for the community that has supported her journey.

One of Liv's most notable qualities is her genuine appreciation for her fans. During WWE meet-and-greet events, she takes the time to listen to their stories, often becoming emotional when fans share how much she has inspired them. Her openness and willingness to connect on a personal level make these moments unforgettable for those who meet her.

Liv's relationship with her fans extends beyond admiration—it's a partnership. She frequently credits the WWE Universe for her success, acknowledging that their support has fueled her career and kept her motivated through challenges. For Liv, being a WWE Superstar is not just about entertaining; it's about making an impact.

As Liv's career has progressed, she has embraced her role as a role model and WWE icon. Her journey from a small-town girl with big dreams to a championship-winning Superstar embodies the essence of resilience and determination. For many fans, especially young women, Liv is a beacon of hope, proving that with hard work and self-belief, anything is possible.

Liv has used her platform to champion inclusivity and empowerment. If it's promoting body positivity, encouraging fans to embrace their individuality, or supporting causes like mental health awareness, she has consistently used her voice to uplift others. Her actions have earned her admiration not just within the WWE Universe but also in the broader world of entertainment.

Beyond the Ring: The Future

As Liv Morgan continues to evolve both personally and professionally, her ambitions extend far beyond the wrestling ring. She envisions a future where she can combine her love for WWE with ventures in fashion, fitness, and entertainment. If it's launching a clothing line, starring in a film, or mentoring the next generation of wrestlers, Liv is determined to leave an indelible mark on the world.

Her story is far from over. For Liv Morgan, the journey beyond the ring is as exciting and unpredictable as her career inside it. The girl from Elmwood Park, New Jersey, who once dreamed of becoming a WWE Superstar, has become a symbol of resilience, authenticity, and limitless potential. And with every step she takes, Liv continues to inspire those who dare to dream big.

Printed in Dunstable, United Kingdom